ONE
DAY
USA

A SELF-PORTRAIT OF AMERICA'S CITIES

EDITED BY
RICHARD AND JUDITH CARVER

IN ASSOCIATION WITH
THE UNITED STATES
CONFERENCE OF MAYORS

HARRY N. ABRAMS, INC., PUBLISHERS, NEW YORK

ONE
DAY
USA

TO THE VISION OF THE EVERYDAY PHOTOGRAPHER

We dedicate this book to Mr. Colin Hall, without whose extraordinary inspiration by virtue of his similar effort, this project would never have been accomplished; and to the thousands of individuals who made the effort to photograph the events of March 20, 1985, because of their interest and commitment to life in their cities. Finally, we would like to dedicate the book to each other. The conversion of this dream to reality came largely as a result of the love and commitment that has made us a team.

Editor: Robert Morton
Assistant Editor: Harriet Whelchel
Designer: Judith Henry

Library of Congress Cataloging-in-Publication Data
One day USA
1. Photography, Artistic. 2. Cities and towns—United States—
Pictorial works. 2. City and town life—United States—
Pictorial works. I. Carver, Richard E., 1938–   . II. Carver,
Judith. III. United States Conference of Mayors. IV. Title:
One day USA.
TR654.069   1986   779′.997309732   86–3620
ISBN 0–8109–0837–9

Times Mirror Books

Printed and bound in Japan

PRECEDING PAGES
This satellite photograph provides a comprehensive view of the United States on March 20, 1985. (Photograph courtesy NOAA/ NESDIS)

LEFT
Savannah, Georgia. A 49ers fan marks the day on a Bryan Street sidewalk. (Joseph Saunders)

CONTENTS

Editor's Note: Included in the book are quotations from speeches by President Reagan and Vice-President Bush, as well as statements on the nature of American cities from U.S. Senators Pete Wilson and Richard G. Lugar (the former mayors of San Diego and Indianapolis) and from the mayors, or former mayors, of San Antonio, Nashville, Newark, Charleston, Boston, Philadelphia, Baltimore, Minneapolis, New York, Savannah, Washington, San Francisco, New Orleans, Atlanta, Tucson, Tampa, Denver, Los Angeles, Kansas City, Detroit, Saint Paul, Lincoln, and New Haven.

Danville, Illinois. North Street (Leslie Woodrum)

Today is Wednesday
March 20, 1985.
It is sunny and
warm outside.
I like Sping.

FOREWORD

You may wonder how a book such as this actually happened. I'm the first to admit that initially it was more of a dream than anything else. Neither my wife, Judy, nor I have ever attempted such a project, and although I myself have taken thousands of photographs all over the world with my faithful Canon, none has ever been published.

The sixteen years that I spent as an elected official in Peoria, Illinois—the last twelve as mayor—nurtured in me a number of ideas and feelings, not the least of which is a deep love for all those things that make up the essence of a city. I also came to be aware that the heart and soul of a community are much easier to capture on film than to attempt to describe in words. This realization led to the idea of creating a twenty-four-hour essay of life in American cities as seen through the lenses of cameras from all over this country.

The challenge for a couple of novices like Judy and me was to persuade people all across America, of all ages and backgrounds, to take their cameras and capture the sense of what their city means to them—in effect to become the real authors of this book.

We chose the first day of spring, March 20, 1985. It was an extraordinary day, because thousands of photographers, amateur and professional, went out with a single idea in mind and took pictures—outstanding pictures, human pictures, beautiful pictures, and some dreadful pictures. But, in all, they produced a fascinating montage, the overriding theme of which was the rich humanity of our cities.

In their search for photographic subjects, the participants in the project crossed barriers, and explored at least for one day the interesting and varied ways of life of the people who live among them, many of whom they never really notice.

Every one of the more than 50,000 color and black-and-white photographs that resulted, however, had something special to say, because each represented a careful, feeling, and personal interpretation of life in our cities. In 200 communities as small as Macomb, Illinois, and as large as Los Angeles, California—from Portland, Maine, to Bellingham, Washington, ranging north to Alaska and west to Hawaii—photographers went out with a mission, remembering that this was their day to tell us about America.

Each city submitted its best ten entries, and from these thousands came the some 320 photographs that have become the contents of this book. It is interesting that among them all are no overtly political images, few that overly glamorize the places shown, and none that took pains to show a city at its worst. These are not pretty postcards, however; they are honest glimpses of real life. There is drama here, but always as a backdrop to the human story of how Americans coexist and cope with life in their cities.

There is no way for us to salute each of the photographers who participated in this great project, except to hope that, as you view this book, you share with us the joy, warmth, and tenderness that they conveyed. America is a magnificent country, whose finest asset is its people. Judy and I truly hope that you will recognize in their efforts just how great and yet how humble are America's cities. We are proud to have made some contribution to that recognition in the realization of our dream, this portrait of twenty-four hours in the lives of our cities.

Richard E. Carver

LEFT
Calumet City, Illinois. Mike Ramirez waits for class to begin at Hoover School. (Michael Zajakowski)

OVERLEAF
Minneapolis, Minnesota. Looking south over the city from the top of the IDS (Investors Diversified Services) Building, at 775 feet high the tallest building in Minneapolis (Mark D. Skapyak)

NIGHT

FROM TOP TO BOTTOM
Tulsa, Oklahoma. American Bowling Congress Tournament, Tulsa Convention Center (Jeff Darby)

Knoxville, Tennessee. Downtown Knoxville from the south bank of the Tennessee River (Gordon A. Parker)

Marion, Ohio, Marion County Courthouse clock, East Center Street (Donald Harty)

Jackson, Mississippi. Galloway Memorial United Methodist Church and the State Capitol Building (Randall Teasley)

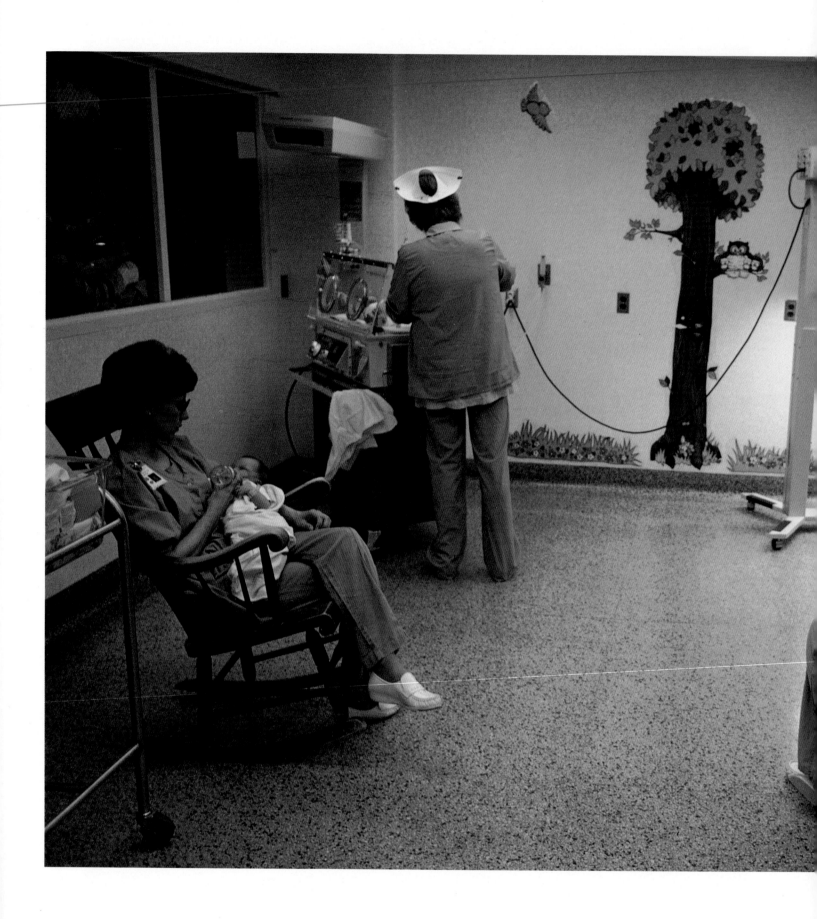

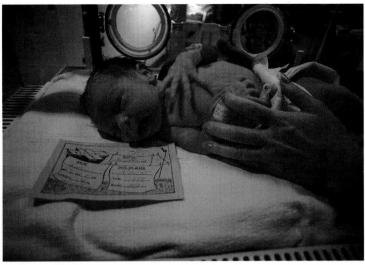

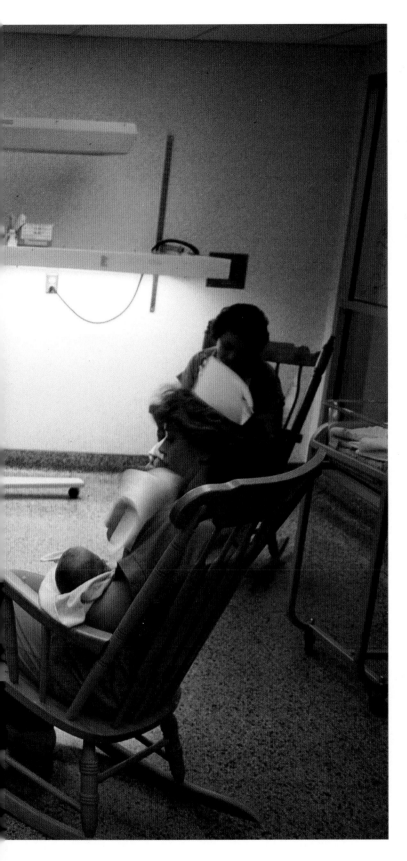

ABOVE
Paducah, Kentucky. Two-hour-old infant, Western Baptist Hospital (Bob Shapiro)

LEFT
Paducah, Kentucky. Western Baptist Hospital (Bob Shapiro)

DAWN

FROM TOP TO BOTTOM
West Allis, Wisconsin. Sunrise from the 92nd Street overpass (William Schalk)

Gulfport, Mississippi. Small craft harbor, downtown Gulfport south of the business district (Pat Sullivan)

New Orleans, Louisiana. Lafayette Cemetery (Leroy Rook)

RIGHT
Santa Barbara, California. Sterns Wharf, East Beach (Irene Bagalio)

OVERLEAF
Bellingham, Washington. Bellingham Bay, Lummi Shore Road (Marina Wiesenbach)

Pompano Beach, Florida. Pompano Pier (Peter Lowery)

PRECEDING PAGES
Philadelphia, Pennsylvania. The Schuylkill River (Robert H. Brown)

Muskegon, Michigan. Hackley Park, downtown Muskegon (Kirk Schultz)

OVERLEAF
Binghamton, New York. Homes in the First Ward (Kirk Van Zandbergen)

Sarasota, Florida. Sarasota Bay (Margo Musial)

Hampton, Virginia. City Hall from across Mill Creek (Christopher Jay Oxley)

OVERLEAF
*Minneapolis, Minnesota. A Chicago Northwestern train passes
through the city to the west of the Mississippi River. (Phill Mueller)*

CLOCKWISE FROM ABOVE
West Haven, Connecticut. Bradley Point (Jean Kaas)

*Aurora, Illinois. Roundhouse, future site of the Aurora
Transportation Center (Jo Fredell Higgins)*

Aurora, Colorado. The Paul Beck Center (Peter D. Newman)

OVERLEAF
*Flint, Michigan. Eastbound cars on Interstate 69 near Irish Road
(John Dickson)*

The . . . final key to a stronger, more prosperous, and stable urban America is a strengthening of basic values through a renewal of community life. People coming together in a spirit of neighborhood is what makes cities worth living in. This spirit sustains businesses and attracts new ones, and keeps faith with the fine traditions of the past while enabling us to build the future with confidence.

RONALD WILSON REAGAN
President of the United States

Dreams are what America is about. It is time for government, when it looks at our present communities, to respect the dreams that flourish there and to help open the windows of opportunity and let in the sunlight of hope, and to step aside to watch these dreams grow into realities.

GEORGE HERBERT WALKER BUSH
Vice-President of the United States

Located on the bluffs of the upper Mississippi River, Saint Paul is a city of great charm and character. It offers its citizens a diverse environment that reflects a proud history, contemporary development, and community commitment to arts, education, and social equality.

Long enjoyed by its residents as an excellent place in which to live, Saint Paul is now recognized nationally as an example of successful urban revitalization. Local optimism is neither subtle nor limited; it is refreshingly obvious. Whether eating a hamburger at Mickey's Diner or listening to a symphony at the superb new Ordway Music Theater, Saint Paulites know their city has superior style.

MAYOR GEORGE LATIMER
Saint Paul, Minnesota

All matters of life fall into one of two categories—dependent or independent. There is no third category. No one in American society exists independently of American cities. The real importance of American cities is that over 230 million people depend on cities for existence as they know it.

MAYOR KENNETH A. GIBSON
Newark, New Jersey

The city of San Antonio is important in its citizens' lives—not because it is the tenth-largest city in the nation, or because of its unique cultural rhythms, but because it has become a metaphor for thousands of families working in union.

These families *are* the city. And our goal is to raise the incomes of a large percentage of those families living below the national median. We have developed a strategy aimed at creating a labor-intensive, high-technology sector—a base for developing jobs containing long career ladders and with higher skills requirements, jobs that provide channels of opportunity for this generation and future generations.

The future of our nation lies in its cities. This union of families—this city—combines tangible optimism with an unceasing effort to invest in the future.

MAYOR HENRY G. CISNEROS
San Antonio, Texas

As mayor of Nashville, I am happy to say that Nashvillians have always taken pride in our beautiful city, whether through photographs or words. Yet recently there has been a special excitement—thanks to many construction and redevelopment projects—that has not been here before. I am most grateful that Nashville is seen as a prospering and growing part of America's cities.

MAYOR RICHARD H. FULTON
Nashville, Tennessee

Cities are the lifeblood of American cooperation and competitiveness. When I was mayor of Indianapolis, we had the amazing opportunity to develop a new type of urban government, which was essential to the emergence of Indianapolis as a great city. As a result of the elimination of redundant and confusing governmental structures, citizens were able to achieve their potential for economic growth and develop a vision of the future for themselves and their children.

RICHARD G. LUGAR
United States Senator
Mayor, Indianapolis, Indiana, 1968–75

CLOCKWISE FROM TOP
Wauwatosa, Wisconsin. North 73rd Street (Ann Craig)

Anchorage, Alaska. Ken Gray celebrates "the liberation of the shadows"
on the campus of the University of Alaska at Anchorage. (Michael Penn)

Philadelphia, Pennsylvania. Parking Authority Badge No. 79 writes a citation
at the corner of 23rd and Chestnut streets. (Mary O'Hara Gregory)

LEFT
Burlington, Vermont. Intersection of Buell Street and South Winooski
Avenue (Gary Clayton-Hall)

OVERLEAF
Toledo, Ohio. Toledo skyline from International Park (D. Peter Bykowski)

ABOVE LEFT
Rochester, Minnesota. Andy Zafft begins his day at the Mayo Clinic with the raising of the U.S. flag. (Deborah Stark)

ABOVE RIGHT
Calumet City, Illinois. Postal clerk Chester Mazur raises the flag outside the Calumet City Post Office. (Michael Zajakowski)

RIGHT
Danbury, Connecticut. Larry Coultrip raises a thirteen-star "Grand Union" flag before leaving for work. This house on Franklin Street, dating from about 1790, is one of the oldest in the city. (Kitt Daone)

OVERLEAF
West New York, New Jersey. Park Avenue between 60th and 61st streets (Frank W. Augustine)

CIVIC CENTER HUDSON DEMOC

LUNES

Fricase de Pollo $1.99 | PICADILLO $1.99
ARROZ Y PAPA   ARROZ Y YUCA

MARTES

CHULETA Frita $1.99 | POLLO bar-ba-Coa $1.99
MORO Y YUCA   Moro y maduro frito

MIERCOLES

PATICA Guisada $1.99 • CHICHARRON de Pollo $1.99
ARROZ Y YUCA   MORO Y PAPITA

KABO
MORO Y MA

MICHELOB Light

SPANISH FOOD
STEAK SAND. $1.99
CUBAN SAND. $1.99
CHARCOAL CHIKEN $.199
BROILED PORKCHOPS.
AMERICAN COFFE 50¢

Open
Abierto

6023

Entrada

ABOVE
Providence, Rhode Island. A shift in the weight of this load of twenty-three tons of salt destined for Cranston, Rhode Island, caused this morning mishap. (Providence Journal Company)

BELOW
Del City, Oklahoma. A morning traffic accident at southeast 28th Street and Sunnylane (Larry Voelker)

CLOCKWISE FROM TOP LEFT
Detroit, Michigan. The Pontchartrain Hotel (Kwabena Shabu)

Meridian, Mississippi. Fireman at the scene of the burned Scottish Rite Temple at 11th and 23rd streets. The building is part of the National Register of Historic Places. (Lila Thomas)

Flint, Michigan. Construction worker, Market Place (Jim Kettler)

FROM TOP TO BOTTOM
Norwich, Connecticut. School crossing guard, Wequonnoc School in the village of Taftville (Debbie Flaum)

Independence, Missouri. Second-grade field trip, Independence Square (Dr. Donald A. Potts)

Lake Charles, Louisiana. School crossing guard, Prien Lake Elementary School (Richard E. Casey)

RIGHT, ABOVE
Terre Haute, Indiana. South 6th Street (Dennis Morgan)

RIGHT, BELOW
Ocala, Florida. Tenth Avenue (Annette Selph)

Roswell, New Mexico. Alumni Memorial Chapel (Aaron Wilson)

ABOVE
Calumet City, Illinois. The Administration Building (Michael Zajakowski)

BELOW
*Nashville, Tennessee. Contractors discuss the laying of the brick for
Nashville's new transit mall on Deaderick Street. (Gary Layda)*

OVERLEAF
*Peoria, Illinois. City Hall and the Twin Towers, downtown
Peoria (Ken Worthington)*

Throughout history, men and women have looked to cities to generate jobs and ideas. Culture and commerce rub shoulders naturally amid the urban environment. Winston Churchill put it well when he said that "men shape cities so that cities can shape men." From London we took our constitutional government and most of our laws. From Rome came one of the world's great religions. Florence gave us Michelangelo, Vienna gave us Freud, New York shared the Broadway musical. And Washington, D.C., believe me, supplies us with an entirely different form of entertainment.

As for San Diego, let's just say it is a pioneer on the frontier of urban livability—a perfect mix of natural climate and human design. San Diego's greatest achievement is not a building or monument. Rather, it is the quality of life that residents extol to visitors. San Diego is a great city—on a human scale.

> PETE WILSON
> United States Senator
> Mayor, San Diego, California, 1971–82

A great city is a celebration of the best of human talent, intelligence, compassion, and spirit. These qualities are reflected daily in the life of the city—in its cultural activities, its educational institutions, its commerce, its neighborhoods, its infrastructure, and in its capacity to find unity for common goals and to preserve diversity for ethnic or religious communities. These qualities certainly have been developed and strengthened in Atlanta, and that is why I am proud to call this beautiful place a great city.

> MAYOR ANDREW YOUNG
> Atlanta, Georgia

San Franciscans think of their city as a very special place: unique in its setting, its people, and its perspectives. Born in a gold rush, destroyed in an earthquake, rebuilt from its ashes, it is forever a city of seekers dreaming new dreams and looking for better lives—and many times, finding them.

> MAYOR DIANNE FEINSTEIN
> San Francisco, California

Washington, D.C., is important to the people who live and visit here because of its abundant cultural life. Its ninety-five neighborhoods are rich in historical significance. Ethnic diversity thrives in the many shops and restaurants offering a variety of goods and cuisines—from African to Chinese, Latin to Caribbean. Neighborhood festivals have become increasingly popular, and they nourish the traditions of the many peoples who call Washington their hometown.

In addition, Washington, D.C., is a unique metropolitan center with a competent, compassionate, and caring work force committed to ensuring a decent quality of life for all of its citizens.

> MAYOR MARION S. BARRY, JR.
> Washington, D.C.

The city is like an oasis in the desert that provides not only replenishment of the body, but also sustenance for the soul. Such is Tucson, a community almost from the time of Christ, a place to love and be loved, a place to realize dreams and awaken hope, a place for the artist and artisan, the king and commoner. This is the Old Pueblo, first city in Arizona, historic city of the West, from which the conquistadores and clergy opened a land all the way to the Pacific Ocean. This is Tucson, city of future, where the expectations for a greater tomorrow are built upon the tradition of a spectacular yesterday. Tucson is a city cosmopolitan, quilt of many designs, a city of light and air amid scenic blessings, a city whose people still know each other by first name.

> MAYOR LEWIS C. MURPHY
> Tucson, Arizona

Cities are the lifeblood of our states and our nation. As the unit of government closest to the people, a city has a dramatic impact on the lives of its citizens and those in the surrounding areas. People rely on their city governments for vital services, without which orderly and peaceful existence would not be possible.

> WILLIAM H. McNICHOLS, JR.
> Mayor, Denver, Colorado, 1969–83

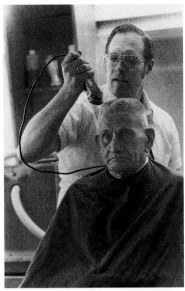

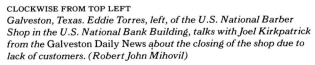

CLOCKWISE FROM TOP LEFT
Galveston, Texas. Eddie Torres, left, of the U.S. National Barber Shop in the U.S. National Bank Building, talks with Joel Kirkpatrick from the Galveston Daily News about the closing of the shop due to lack of customers. (Robert John Mihovil)

Newark, Ohio. Vaughn Brothers Barber Shop, 4th Street (Chris Kasson)

Middletown, Connecticut. Carlos Spinoza serves breakfast at Hall's Diner on Main Street. (Laura Radin)

Danville, Illinois. "Dr. Shine" in front of Deutsch Brothers in the Downtown Mall (Steve Elmore)

Bountiful, Utah. Don Carmack of Carmack's, South Main Street (James E. Child)

Salt Lake City, Utah. Promised Valley Playhouse, South State Street
(William Cupit)

*Providence, Rhode Island. Donna De Santis directs traffic on West
Exchange Street, construction site of the new Fire and Police
Communications Headquarters Building. (James A. Egan)*

OVERLEAF
*Rochester, Minnesota. Dr. Martin Adson makes his rounds, St. Mary's
Hospital. (Jim Welch)*

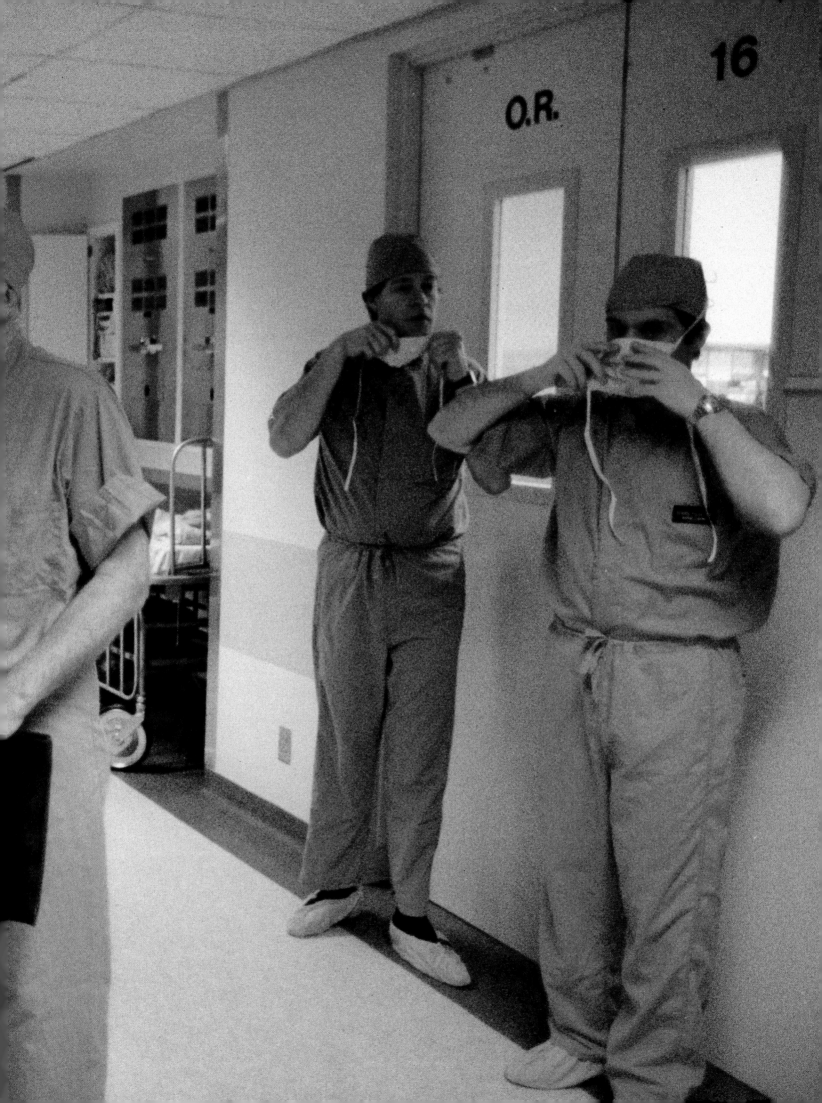

CLOCKWISE FROM TOP LEFT
Toledo, Ohio. Willow Cemetery, in the suburb of Oregon (Leslie Sponseller)

Everett, Massachusetts. Everett Industries, south Everett (Neal L. Whitman)

Columbus, Georgia. Government Center, 10th Street (City Employees)

RIGHT
Elkhart, Indiana. West Franklin Street (Matt Stokely)

OVERLEAF
Pasadena, California. Old and new Pasadena, reflected in a building at the corner of Colorado Boulevard and Arroyo Parkway (Charles Eickele)

CLOCKWISE FROM TOP LEFT
Newark, New Jersey. Serta Mattress Company (David Booker)

Waukesha, Wisconsin. Best Florist on East Moreland, Waukesha's main street (Lisa G. Huff)

Fitchburg, Massachusetts. Releasing the swans, Coggshall Park (Kathy Coulson)

Hagerstown, Maryland. City workers plant Christmas trees in Washington Square for next year. (Donna Graffunder)

PRECEDING PAGES
Albany, New York. Empire State Plaza (Joseph Smith)

Bloomington, Indiana. Courthouse Square (Doug Benedict)

Lakewood, Ohio. Signs of spring are evident in the flower-bordered walkway of this Clifton Park home. (Jeff Weseling)

FROM TOP TO BOTTOM
Lexington, Massachusetts. Spring plants for sale at Lexington Gardens (Natalie Robinson)

Portage, Michigan. Purple crocuses, City Hall (Donna McKenna)

Mount Lebanon, Pennsylvania. Johnston Florist, Washington Road (Joan G. Ramsey)

People talk about the relationships between man and nature. In a city, we are in a primarily man-made environment in which we face ourselves—in remnants of our past and constant reminders of the need for rehabilitation to reshape our future.

Eighty-two percent of the residential structures in Minneapolis are still single-family homes that are owner-occupied. It's the Midwest ethic: everyone deserves to own a home with a plot of land to garden sometime during his or her life. We are lucky in Minneapolis to have enough land near lakes or other amenities to accommodate this ethic within a central city.

But what is most important in Minneapolis is our sense of community. "Things" have got to matter less than caring for others. We are fortunate to have many kinds of organizations through which people can contribute to a common cause.

I tend to care most about what is happening to our youth. The crazy thing is that they tend to receive less coordinated attention than our senior citizens—even though they represent the future of our community.

MAYOR DONALD M. FRASER
Minneapolis, Minnesota

A city provides its citizens a sense of community. It is a center of commerce, culture, entertainment, and most important of all, a place for people to live, work, grow, and interact with each other, expressing their diversity and their unity. A city takes the uniqueness of individual neighborhoods and fashions a distinctive and dynamic wholeness. A city allows people to enjoy life through its culture, to express their creativity and talent, to raise families in a stable environment, and to voice their citizenship through active participation in city decisions. A city endows its people with a sense of their heritage, with purpose for the present and opportunities for a vital and robust future. A city enables its citizens to share in new and enriching experiences and to say with pride to others, "This is where we live."

HELEN BOOSALIS
Mayor, Lincoln, Nebraska, 1975–83

The importance of the city of Los Angeles to the people who live here can be summed up in one word: community. Even though its boundaries spread for miles, from the mountains to the desert to the beaches along the Pacific coast, Los Angeles is still not too big to manage the task of being an international township for people from all over the world.

The ethnic diversity of Los Angeles gives the city not only a colorful palette for its human canvas, but also a richness in culture unmatched by almost every other major city in the United States, and, despite its size, people worldwide have been able to come here and quickly realize that "L.A.'s the place" they can call home.

MAYOR TOM BRADLEY
Los Angeles, California

Some Americans consider New York City to be a place apart—yet to people all around the world, New York City *is* America. Today, just as centuries ago, a quarter of all New Yorkers are foreign-born. Today, New York City is again welcoming waves of newcomers and helping them along into the mainstream of American life. Like it or not, New York is the city that sums up the American Dream, that holds the key to the restless, unceasing energy of American life. Certainly we have Broadway's glitter and restaurants of every national taste, magnificent museums and skyscrapers and huge public works, a harbor full of history symbolized by majestic Lady Liberty—but look closer and you will see that what makes New York unique transcends all this. It is an idea that here is a city always wide open to new faces and new ideas; a city that beckons those whose needs and ambitions cannot be fulfilled anywhere else; a city that has roused people from all over this country and the world to come here to try to make their mark—to write the great book, to make it big on Wall Street, to win a world championship. Here those needs and ambitions are in collision, every hour of every day. And the result? Something larger than life; something always just a little different; but something indispensable.

MAYOR EDWARD I. KOCH
New York, New York

The twentieth century has brought enormous change to our American way of life, and cities like Baltimore have proved highly adaptable to that change. Baltimore has continued to provide a physical, economic, and social framework for the lives of its residents and, to a greater or lesser extent, the lives of residents of the metropolitan area and the state of Maryland. Our neighborhoods, stronger than ever, are a source of identity and diversity. Downtown has become everyone's neighborhood. From the Orioles to the Baltimore Symphony, our cultural institutions are benefiting from this newly strengthened urban focus. The pride Baltimoreans feel in the resurgence of their city, though not quite measurable, has made its influence felt in every walk of life.

MAYOR WILLIAM DONALD SCHAEFER
Baltimore, Maryland

The city is the cornerstone of civilization as we know it.

Cities are centers of energy, imagination, and creativity, headquarters for commerce and industry, education and the arts. They also are the focal point for our most pressing social problems.

We can best judge a society by its cities—by the height of achievement reached within them and by the quality and intensity of the attention they devote to their problems.

MAYOR COLEMAN A. YOUNG
Detroit, Michigan

Charleston has preserved its past through time and will continue to protect this rich heritage of our built environment. This is a workable and attractive city because of the self-renewing spirit and cooperation of its varied people. Charleston of the 1980s will be remembered as a place where people of different races, backgrounds, and economic interests met, talked, and worked together to create a dynamic synergism and the quality of life that makes this city so irresistible.

MAYOR JOSEPH P. RILEY, JR.
Charleston, South Carolina

Cities are personified in the life force of their citizens. The bricks and mortar of which cities are built are but empty shells without the vibrancy of their inhabitants.

Cities directly reflect the quality of life—and the essence—of the population. Cities are the focal point of their residents' daily lives, providing identification, structure, and roots. The physical city, at any given time, is indeed a compilation of the spirit, dreams, and accomplishments of those whose prior efforts have created the present city entity. And the basic integrity of cities lies in their service as this thread of continuity and support for all generations.

If love can be extended to inanimate construction, then the greatest cities are those which engender the love of their citizens, and Philadelphia is indeed a wonderful example of a great city.

MAYOR W. WILSON GOODE
Philadelphia, Pennsylvania

The spirit of Boston reflects the spirit of its neighborhoods and people. From Faneuil Hall to the revitalized downtown area, Boston represents a unique blend of the past and the future. Keenly aware of Boston's historical importance as the birthplace of liberty, its citizens view participation in the democratic process as the continuation of Boston's special legacy. Due to its great cultural diversity, Boston has evolved into a city of people from all walks of life and from all ethnic groups, sharing equally in the new spirit of their city. Boston is the city of the future with a significant historical past.

MAYOR RAYMOND L. FLYNN
Boston, Massachusetts

Our city is growing because we have a strong commitment to economic development that strikes a balance between industrial growth and the environment, commerce and the community, progress and tradition.

MAYOR BOB MARTINEZ
Tampa, Florida

FROM TOP TO BOTTOM
Bellingham, Washington. Mrs. Joshua Lines, poet, born September 24, 1886, on the porch of her home, where she has lived since 1914 (Alice V. Anderson)

Euclid, Ohio. Lake Erie, by the Euclid Clubhouse (Donna M. Riedel)

Pittsburgh, Pennsylvania. Shadyside Market, Walnut Street (R. Keller)

Topeka, Kansas. Band practice, Municipal Auditorium (Thad Allton)

Galveston, Texas. John Garlington surfs in the gulf waters, near 49th Street. (Robert John Mihovil)

RIGHT
Santa Barbara, California. Corner of Cabrillo and Bath streets (Irene Bagalio)

OVERLEAF
Sioux Falls, South Dakota. Cindy Kramer, left, 19, and Deanna Martin, 21, take a ride with Kramer's team of horses in the western section of Sioux Falls. (Dean Curtis)

ABOVE
Eau Claire, Wisconsin. Elevated view of Park Place along the Chippewa River (James Maylin Erdman)

BELOW
Daly City, California. Recess, Daniel Webster School (Christy Dowd)

Corpus Christi, Texas. Corpus Christi's port is the deepest in Texas. In this photograph, a Korean vessel is loaded with grain bound for Ethiopia. (Jose A. Cano)

OVERLEAF
Albany, New York. Rehabilitation project on Swan Street (John Googas)

CLOCKWISE FROM TOP LEFT
Lansing, Michigan. The State Capitol (Donald Norris)

Artesia, California. California First Bank, Gridley Road north of 187th Street (Albert Little)

North Tonawanda, New York. This late nineteenth-century mansion is among the homes built by prosperous lumber barons who occupied the area at the time. (Joseph Brzezinski)

Denver, Colorado. Montage view of the Grant-Humphreys mansion (Barbara Keating)

Washington, D.C. The White House (Richard D. Corley)

Macomb, Illinois. The Chandler Park Arch (Debbie L. Coutre)

New Rochelle, New York. Presbyterian Church, Pintard Avenue near Main Street (David Finn)

Cincinnati, Ohio. Downtown Cincinnati (Gary Tepe)

Los Angeles, California. Seventh and Broadway, downtown Los Angeles (Chris Morland)

ABOVE
Portsmouth, Virginia. Glascow Street (Mike Williams, The Virginia-Pilot/Ledger-Star)

BELOW
Aurora, Illinois. Looking south at the corner of Galena Boulevard and Stolp Avenue. The left half of the photograph is a reflection from the window of a parking garage. (Stuart Bradley)

ABOVE
Boca Raton, Florida. Carol Seid at the Palmetto Park Road Shopping Center (Anita Heidelback)

RIGHT
Nashville, Tennessee. Castner Knott department store, Church Street (Gary Layda)

FROM TOP TO BOTTOM
Wilmington, North Carolina. Riverfront, Water Street (Joyce L. Morrison)

Idaho Falls, Idaho. Tautphaus Park (Patricia Crockett)

Sandy City, Utah. Snowbird Ski Resort remains open as late as July 1 every year. (Jan Christenson)

LEFT
La Crosse, Wisconsin. View of La Crosse from Hedge Hog Bluff (Daniel M. Wilson)

OVERLEAF
Provo, Utah. Cougar Stadium, Brigham Young University (Liisa Gardner)

Novato, California. Lenten Midweek Eucharist, St. Francis of Assisi Episcopal Church (Martha L. Fritz)

Alameda, California. Victorian restoration, Regent and Clay streets (Lola Curtis)

CLOCKWISE FROM LOWER LEFT
*Fresno, California. Acrobats, sculpture by Clement Renzi, Fresno
City College (Gert Wilkinson)*

*Chula Vista, California. The Music Machine, a group of students from
Bonita Vista High School, perform in front of City Hall. (Mark Cox)*

Boynton Beach, Florida. Southwest 2nd Avenue (Amy Golia)

Irvine, California. Space Net, Deerfield Community Park (Paul M. Sanchez)

ABOVE
Lima, Ohio. The town square from the roof of the Huntington Bank Building (Steven G. Fisher)

BELOW
Inkster, Michigan. Inkster Library and the Twin Towers (Raymond Shaw)

*New Orleans, Louisiana. Corner of Camp and Gravier streets.
(Marilyn Bowes McQueary)*

FROM TOP TO BOTTOM
Springfield, Missouri. Springfield Airport (John E. Davidson)

*Coral Springs, Florida. View from the roof of the Sunrise Towers
Building, North University Drive (Virginia Tooze)*

Montclair, New Jersey. Edgemont Park, Valley Road (Carol Dandy)

Reno, Nevada. Sign repair, Reno Hilton Hotel and Casino (Trent Saviers)

Biloxi, Mississippi. Two guests model their spring hats in the courtyard of Mary Mahoney's Old French House Restaurant. (Eileen Mahoney-Pitalo)

Hawthorne, California. Yodarkis Gouea and Cyndy Torcynski mow lawns on 137th Street. (Oscar Talleda)

Key West, Florida. Smather's Beach (Jeffrey Cardenas)

Sunnyvale, California. Cape Cod Village (Gene Gear)

Fort Lauderdale, Florida. Canal by Pier 66 Hotel and Marina (Donna and Ken Chesler)

West Palm Beach, Florida. Saint Ann's Catholic Church, North Olive Avenue, with Northbridge office building, North Flagler Drive, in the background. (Linda A. Jaquith)

Charleston, South Carolina. Vintage Charleston architecture, Church Street (Binky Maness)

AFTERNOON

CLOCKWISE FROM TOP LEFT
Maui County, Hawaii. Kapuna Auntie Inez Ashdown at Heritage
Gardens of Iao Valley. Kapuna is Hawaiian for elder. (Margo Berdeshevsky)

Toledo, Ohio. Anderson's General Store (Sue Keyser)

Garden Grove, California. Strawberry stand, Chapman Avenue (Mike DeGree)

PRECEDING PAGES
Philadelphia, Pennsylvania. Italian market, 9th and Catherine streets (Bruce Stromberg)

Evanston, Illinois. Sunbather on Church Street (Tom Cruze)

ABOVE
Miami Beach, Florida. Lincoln Road Mall (Fred Mooke)

BELOW
Pasadena, California. Pasadena City Hall (Geraint O. Smith)

Terre Haute, Indiana. South 5th Street (Dennis Morgan)

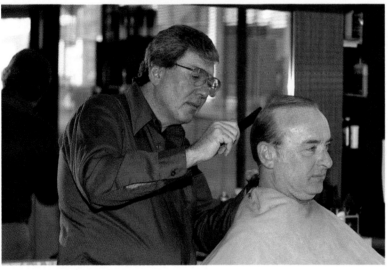

CLOCKWISE FROM TOP LEFT
*Terre Haute, Indiana. AMAX Mine, Highway 70 east of the city
(Myrtle Carpenter)*

*Danbury, Connecticut. Lunch break at the Danbury Hat Company
(Jenine I. Michaud)*

*Lexington, Massachusetts. A quilting stitch brings this log cabin quilt,
the culmination of a winter's work, to near completion. Rena
Wischhusen's project began in adult education classes in the public
school system. (Fred Wischhusen)*

*Kokomo, Indiana. Walt Moss in his barbershop, corner of North Main
and Taylor streets (Donald G. McKillip)*

*Hawthorne, California. Kenneth, of Kenneth's Barbershop,
Hawthorne Boulevard (Ken Steinhardt)*

Anchorage, Alaska. The Hunt Building (Steve Armbrust)

FROM TOP TO BOTTOM

Rockford, Illinois. Midway Theater, East State Street (Nels Akerlund)

Jacksonville, Florida. Aerial view of Jacksonville and the St. John's River from Friendship Park (Judy Jacobsen)

Chula Vista, California. Aerial view of City Hall (Mark Cox)

Chicago Heights, Illinois. Senior citizens attend exercise class in the Chicago Heights Park District Building. (Ted Skowronski)

Lynn, Massachusetts. Dance Central, Central Avenue (Jim Baldwin)

FROM TOP TO BOTTOM
Hazleton, Pennsylvania. Hazleton National Bank, Broad and Laurel streets (Mary Tucci)

Birmingham, Alabama. Birmingham Green, 20th Street, downtown Birmingham (Ann Adams)

Jackson, Mississippi. Capital Street, in front of the governor's mansion (Mary Powell Jabaley)

Victoria, Texas. Old Victoria County Courthouse (James Langdon)

ABOVE
Peoria, Illinois. Intersection of Jefferson and Hamilton streets (Henry J. Blackwell)

BELOW
Boston, Massachusetts. A mounted policeman patrols the restored area of downtown Boston.
(Lynnelle Corley-Piercy)

Farmington, New Mexico. Navajo woman making fry bread,
downtown Farmington (Stephanie Starkey)

Lima, Ohio. The mirrored surface of the Blue Cross Building creates both a self-portrait of the photographer and a reflected image of the new Civic Center. (Andrew M. Archer)

Hayward, California. Mission Boulevard, north of A Street (Donald Eric Buchholz)

FROM TOP TO BOTTOM
*Franklin Township, New Jersey. Cricket Store, corner of Amwell
Road and DeMott Lane, Middlebush Historic District (Lola Kurland
Gerchick)*

Bristol, Connecticut. Main Street, downtown Bristol (John Schissler)

*Schenectady, New York. Jay Street Mall, State and Jay streets
(Gregory Guzzo)*

Lynn, Massachusetts. Lynn Public Library (Dan Coffey)

I have had many chances in life to be something other than a mayor, but there is—to me—no finer calling in public service than to run a city. Cities are where the action is, and where the problems are. If our nation is to be one in which all men are equal, cities are where this goal must be achieved, not in Washington or in Congress or the White House, not in the state house, but in city hall, U.S.A.

Being a mayor was the most exciting and glorious experience of my life. I would not swap my eight terms as mayor for anything I have ever seen or experienced, either in public or private life—not for wealth or power. We were able, in a little less than two decades, to change the face of our city, to ameliorate the lot of thousands of our people, to provide better housing, and to improve our school system. With the help of a community whose people had risen to the challenge, we were able to begin to raise the quality of life of those people who had been tucked away in the ghettos and the slums, receiving their welfare checks or their pension checks, ignored for generations, despite all of their problems, both physical and mental. But it was only a start, and the job in New Haven, as in America, is not nearly completed.

RICHARD C. LEE
Mayor, New Haven, Connecticut, 1954–69

The Mile High City of Denver serves as home to over 500,000 individuals who work and relax beside the beauty of the Rocky Mountains. A growing city, Denver offers unique amenities that meet the needs of varied interests and life-styles. And although Denver has become a very cosmopolitan area, its people still have the same independent spirit of Denver residents from the pioneering days, Denver is more than a place in which to live, it is a way of life.

MAYOR FEDERICO PEÑA
Denver, Colorado

Our network of cities across America was, and remains today, the bedrock of the American system. It was in our cities that Americans joined together for the common good to build their homes, their schools, their businesses, and to raise their families. Our cities were not delineated by royal charters, by conquests or claims, or by boundaries on a map; they came into existence through the choice of people. Savannah is here by that choice and is today a strong, vibrant, and beautiful city ready for the future.

MAYOR JOHN P. ROUSAKIS
Savannah, Georgia

New Orleans has never been just "a great city." It is a neighborhood, families exploring the French Quarter, a father and his children sharing the same streetcar ride to work and school. New Orleans is a living example of the past, present, and future greatness of America.

MAYOR ERNEST N. MORIAL
New Orleans, Louisiana

Kansas City, Missouri, like all cities, infuses vitality, excitement, and a sense of human values into the life of its region.

Cities are essential to the creation of those amenities that make life special, that transcend the modern workaday world, and that bring a feeling of shared humanity to every individual.

In concrete terms, Kansas City offers all who come here great art and music, theater and ballet, professional sports, genuine jazz, the best barbecue around, beautiful parks and boulevards, recreational opportunities, fine residential neighborhoods, and the excitement of a booming modern city.

Kansas City is the home of the 1985 World Champion Kansas City Royals.

MAYOR RICHARD L. BERKELEY
Kansas City, Missouri

Boulder, Colorado. Local musician, Pearl Street Pedestrian Mall (Sandra Hale)

*Lakewood, Ohio. Yesterday's Antiques, Detroit Avenue
(Ruth Ann Eckart)*

*Modesto, California. John Brinks of J & H Auto Dismantlers with the
best of the more than 3,000 wheels and rims J & H has in stock. (John
Haley Scott)*

Bellflower, California. Statue of Liberty, Simms Park (Don Whitney)

Schenectady, New York. Statue of Liberty, Liberty Park (Jim Beswick)

ABOVE
North Little Rock, Arkansas. Downtown North Little Rock from atop the Rogers Building (Charles G. Wetzler)

BELOW
Evansville, Indiana. Ohio River from the overlook at Riverfront Park (William F. Norris, Jr.)

Altoona, Pennsylvania. Alto Tower, 17th Street (Helen Boyer)

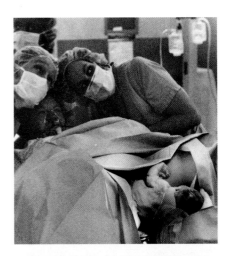

CLOCKWISE FROM TOP LEFT
Lancaster, California. Amanda Rose Johnson is born at 2:26 P.M. at Antelope Valley Hospital Medical Center. Mother Andrea Johnson and nurses watch the procedure through a mirror at upper right, out of the photograph. (Lee Bergthold)

Reno, Nevada. Newlyweds Terry and Dolly Johnes from Oregon pose on North Virginia Street. (Elke Morris)

Concord, New Hampshire. Judge Hugh Bownes, First Circuit U.S. Court of Appeals, on Pleasant Street (Nancer Ballard)

LEFT
Minneapolis, Minnesota. Funeral of Edward P. (Eddie) Schwartz, Temple Israel (Wally Kammann)

OVERLEAF
Meridian, Mississippi. Air National Guard jets, Key Field (Robert B. Deen, Jr.)

ABOVE
Monroe, Louisiana. Forsythe Park, Forsythe Avenue (Robert Ragland)

BELOW
Galveston, Texas. Gulf view, San Luis Hotel (Thomas Bednarek)

Annapolis, Maryland. Spa Creek (Thomas J. Curley)

Saint Paul, Minnesota. Saint Paul skyline, Harriet Island (Bernice E. Westlund)

Gulfport, Mississippi. Saddlehorn Leather Shop, downtown Gulfport (Pat Sullivan)

OVERLEAF
Denver, Colorado. The International Livestock Show is held each year in the Denver Coliseum. (Jay Di Lorenzo)

ABOVE
Lake Charles, Louisiana. North Beach (Mike Fruge)

BELOW
Redondo Beach, California. Knob Hill (Timm Eubanks)

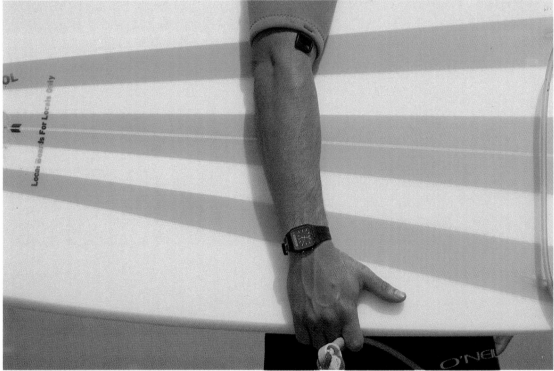

ABOVE
Maui County, Hawaii. Jumping ship off the island of Maui (Bill F. Eger)

BELOW
Corpus Christi, Texas. Surfer, Padre Island (Cynthia Jean Garza)

Fitchburg, Massachusetts. Fitchburg High School, Wallace Avenue (Alden Sherwin)

Denton, Texas. Denton County Courthouse (Dane W. Bass)

Bellingham, Washington. Butch Bua repairs nets on the Friendship. *(Dave Walker)*

*Baton Rouge, Louisiana. Crawfish, Tony's Seafood, Plank Road
(Joe S. Costa III)*

ABOVE
Boulder, Colorado. Farrand Field, University of Colorado (Martin Goodman)

BELOW
Lynn, Massachusetts. Goldfish Pond, Lafayette Park (Jody Scioletti)

Alexandria, Virginia. In Alexandria's historic Market Square, Colonial military drills are reenacted. A young visitor stands in the foreground. (Nina Tisara, Alexandria Tourist Council)

North Miami, Florida. Northwest Baptist Church playground, 135th Street and 10th Avenue (Catherine Shaffer)

La Mirada, California. Behringer Park (Ed Gillum)

OVERLEAF
Evansville, Indiana. Madison Street and Garvin (Eric Hassler)

FROM TOP TO BOTTOM
Coral Springs, Florida. Mullins Park (Virginia Tooze)

Lauderhill, Florida. Castle Garden Condominium (Hal Rackin)

*Muskogee, Oklahoma. Girls' Softball Complex, Memorial Park
(John C. Spinks)*

RIGHT
*West Palm Beach, Florida. Giorries Johnson peers into the dugout
during a spring training game between the Montreal Expos and the
Baltimore Orioles at West Palm Municipal Stadium. (Tina Newmark)*

OVERLEAF
*La Crosse, Wisconsin. Construction continues on a new parking ramp,
3rd Street between State and Main. (Mark Anderson)*

CLOCKWISE FROM TOP LEFT
Bountiful, Utah. Bountiful Park, at the crossing of West and North streets (Tom Turner)

Elizabeth, New Jersey. Broad Street, central business district (Harold Hasan)

Normal, Illinois. School crossing guard, Oakdale Elementary School, Woodland and Oakland avenues (Trudy Wollenschlager)

Norman, Oklahoma. Andrews Park (Dennis Borycki)

Gainesville, Florida. Pumping gas, 13th Street and 6th Avenue (Thomas McKerchen)

Bloomington, Indiana. Construction site of the Justice Building, corner of 7th and College streets (Sidney Sander)

Denver, Colorado. La Paz 10 Pool Hall (Javan Bayer)

Canton, Ohio. West Tuscarawas Street (Richard L. Mercorelli)

Garden Grove, California. Garden Grove High School
(Mark Thiessen)

Lexington, Massachusetts. Stop 'N Shop parking lot, corner of
Bedford Street and Worthen Road (Natalie Robinson)

OVERLEAF
Altoona, Pennsylvania. Shift change at the Conrail yard
(Larry G. McKee)

Savannah, Georgia. River Street (Jimmy Lee Shupe)

Independence, Missouri. Independence Square (Mrs. Mary May)

East Orange, New Jersey. Annette Passmore and Michael Lloyd in front of East Orange City Hall (Ernie Johnston, Jr.)

Iowa City, Iowa. Old Capitol rally (Michelle Martin)

ABOVE
Sunnyvale, California. Sunnyvale Technology Centre, Ross Avenue (Gene Gear)

BELOW
Hialeah, Florida. The Mayor's Arbor, Hialeah Park (Joel B. McEachern)

Marion, Ohio. Harding Memorial, Delaware Avenue (Al Tozer)

ABOVE
Knoxville, Tennessee. The spring foliage along Dogwood Trail in the suburb of Fountain City inspired area residents to christen the neighborhood "Fantasy Land." (Digby G. Seymour)

BELOW
Newton, Massachusetts. City Hall (David Smilg)

Lubbock, Texas. Students stroll through Memorial Circle on the campus of Texas Tech University, open since 1925, with an enrollment of 23,000. (Vaughn Hendrie)

CLOCKWISE FROM TOP LEFT
Binghamton, New York. Broome County Courthouse, Court Street, downtown Binghamton (Joseph F. Fabrizio)

Buffalo, New York. Corner of Main and Church streets. (Henryk Jarosz)

Indianapolis, Indiana. Monument Circle (Georgia McGuire)

Mansfield, Ohio. Vasbinder Fountain, downtown Mansfield (name withheld by request)

RIGHT
Maple Heights, Ohio. View from rear of Lear Siegler's aircraft component parts plant, Broadway and Rockside Road (Steve Romanik)

Springfield, Missouri. Many of the older houses in the area of Walnut Street are being torn down to make way for new development projects. The high-rise building at left is named for John Q. Hammons, a local developer. (John E. Davidson)

San Antonio, Texas. The Alamo (Carol Kelley)

Manchester, New Hampshire. Merrimack Street, in the Historic District (Charles A. De Grandpre)

Allentown, Pennsylvania. Chestnut Street (Janice Geider)

Appleton, Wisconsin. College Avenue (Ted Zolkowski)

Canton, Ohio. Downtown on the square — the tower of the Stark County Courthouse is reflected through the Harter Bank window. (Terry Horner)

FROM TOP TO BOTTOM
Nashville, Tennessee. The Parthenon (Robert M. Vantrease)

Lancaster, California. Apollo Park (Darlene Sprunger)

Saint Petersburg, Florida. Picnic 'N Pops concert, Straub Park (Howard C. O'Reilly)

York, Pennsylvania. Chamber of Commerce/Legg Mason Building, City Square (Bill Schintz)

Hialeah, Florida. St. John's School (Bill Held)

ABOVE
Hartford, Connecticut. The Ghetto Brothers, Main Street (Michael Meucci)

BELOW
Anchorage, Alaska. Athabascans, behind Rexall's, 4th Avenue between
D and E streets (Trent Swanson)

CLOCKWISE FROM TOP LEFT
Key West, Florida. Captain Tony Terracino, proprietor of Captain Tony's Saloon — the original Sloppy Joe's Bar — gives his daughter, Josephina, and granddaughter Samantha a ride on the fourteen-foot hammerhead shark mounted in the bar. (Jeffrey Cardenas)

Augusta, Georgia. Young girl on Greene Street (B. Newman Bancraft)

Farmers Branch, Texas. Mallon Park (Robert Asher)

Alhambra, California. On the way home from Northrup School (Jesse Chen)

ABOVE
Bellflower, California. Caruthers Park (Don Whitney)

OVERLEAF
Altoona, Pennsylvania. Ninth Street (Bonita Friedenberger)

FROM TOP TO BOTTOM
Cheyenne, Wyoming. Lions Park (Craig Pindell)

*Rockford, Illinois. Riverview Ice House, Rock River, downtown
Rockford (Harlan K. Shank)*

*Des Plaines, Illinois. Library, Oakton Community College
(Karen Henrikson)*

LEFT
Kettering, Ohio. Ernst Park (Peter Doyle)

OVERLEAF
Danbury, Connecticut. Fire on Turner Road (Kurt Beck)

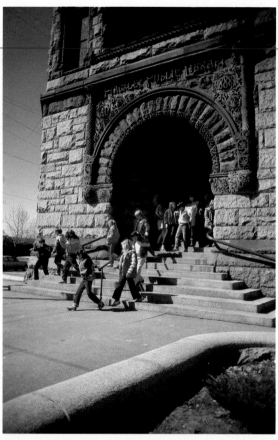

CLOCKWISE FROM TOP LEFT
Charleston, South Carolina. Church Street (Brenda Pulcino)

Muskegon, Michigan. Hackley Public Library (Edward E. Gilmore)

*Parma, Ohio. St. Josaphat Ukrainian Catholic Church, State Road
(Tony Mauser)*

Newton, Massachusetts. The spire of Newton City Hall (Gary Baird)

Santa Barbara, California. Santa Barbara Community College Stadium (Rick Rew)

FROM TOP TO BOTTOM

Rockville, Maryland. Linda Pomerantz in her home at Surry Court
(David Pomerantz)

Portland, Maine. Artist Stuart Ross painting on Fore Street
(John Ferris)

Garland, Texas. A worker checks an electronic circuit board.
(Steve Knaggs)

*Middletown, Connecticut. View of the waterfront and downtown Middletown
from the grounds of the Connecticut Valley Hospital (Sarah Holle)*

Longmont, Colorado. Great Western Sugar Company (Roger Drotar)

North Tonawanda, New York. Fisherman's Park on the Niagara River (Joseph Brzezinski)

Tempe, Arizona. Kyrene Junior High School (Melissa Jameson)

Cape Girardeau, Missouri. Cape Girardeau Bridge, spanning the Mississippi River (Margaret Ostendorf)

*Jersey City, New Jersey. Entrance to the Holland Tunnel, downtown
Jersey City (ATAVA)*

OVERLEAF
Northglenn, Colorado. E. B. Rains, Jr., Memorial Park (Sue Johnson)

EVENING

CLOCKWISE FROM TOP LEFT
Kettering, Ohio. Ernst Park (Peter Doyle)

Euclid, Ohio. Sims Park, on Lake Erie (Robert Chitwood)

*Evansville, Indiana. Morton Avenue, part of the Washington Avenue
Historic District (Tony Kirves)*

Buena Park, California. City Hall (Lou Ruiz)

North Miami, Florida. Bayshore Park Boardwalk (Susan M. Payette)

*Mankato, Minnesota. North Front Street, part of Old Town
(David H. Malcomson, Jr.)*

San Bernardino, California. San Bernardino County Courthouse (Lynn M. Darnell)

FROM TOP TO BOTTOM
Quincy, Illinois. Quincy Bridge (Bruce Helmreich)

*Baton Rouge, Louisiana. Mississippi River Bridge, River Road, near
the Louisiana State University campus (Nancy Q. Kirk)*

*Torrance, California. Its one-and-a-half-mile stretch of beach has
earned Torrance the unofficial nickname "Beach City." (J. Walker Owens)*

ABOVE
Bountiful, Utah. Corner of South and East streets (James E. Child)

BELOW
Wilkes-Barre, Pennsylvania. Public Square (Michelle Renee Boyer)

Mankato, Minnesota. North Front Street (David H. Malcomson, Jr.)

Natchez, Mississippi. Boarding the riverboats, Silver Street (Mark L. Thompson)

Philadelphia, Pennsylvania. City skyline from the PATCO train on the Ben Franklin Bridge, crossing the Delaware River (Joseph F. Mulhearn, Jr.)

Baltimore, Maryland. Harbor Place, in Baltimore's inner harbor, is the site of 130 shops and restaurants. (Richard Lippendaly)

ABOVE
Fort Lauderdale, Florida. Spring Break, Fort Lauderdale Beach
(Tom Weber)

BELOW
Suffolk, Virginia. Chuckatuck Creek (Karla Smith)

CLOCKWISE FROM TOP LEFT
Maple Heights, Ohio. Carol's Maple Leaf Tavern, Broadway at Libby Road (Jim Terlop)

Maui County, Hawaii. Condominium Hotel (Nathan Cobert)

Bellingham, Washington. Broadway Park (Rod del Pozo)

Peoria, Illinois. Thompson Food Basket, North Knoxville, in the East Bluff section of the city (Ralph Fairchild)

Highland Park, Illinois. First National Bank Building, Central Avenue (Mike H. Schmitt)

FROM TOP TO BOTTOM
Baldwin Park, California. The San Bernardino Freeway from the Athol Street Bridge (Eugene A. Pinheiro)

Kankakee, Illinois. View of the city from a River Street high rise (Richard G. Buss)

Bellingham, Washington. Champion Street, downtown Bellingham (John LaFarge)

Kirkwood, Missouri. An Amtrak train pulls into the Kirkwood train station. (James Brazee)

CLOCKWISE FROM TOP LEFT

Albuquerque, New Mexico. View of the city from the mayor's home (Tom C. Tennies)

Las Cruces, New Mexico. The Las Cruces Sun News *neon sign sets off an aerial view of the city. (Janice Corbin)*

Birmingham, Alabama. East-west railroad tracks, 21st Street viaduct at 1st Avenue (Jim Willett)

Allentown, Pennsylvania. View of Allentown and the Lehigh River, taken from Hanover Acres (John Dal Pezzo)

LEFT
Burlington, Vermont. Pearl Street (Richard A. Doran)

OVERLEAF
Paducah, Kentucky. Kennedy Funeral Home, South 6th Street (Bob Shapiro)

CLOCKWISE FROM TOP LEFT
New London, Connecticut. Green Street (Craig Collerette)

Topeka, Kansas. St. Joseph's Church (Bob Bellinder)

West Allis, Wisconsin. Corner of 77th and National (William Schalk)

Decatur, Illinois. Civil War Memorial, Central Park (William T. Haenny, Jr.)

Manchester, New Hampshire. City Hall (Robert K. Legg)

CLOCKWISE FROM TOP LEFT
Charleston, West Virginia. Ninety-year-old Walter Gardner stands in the lobby of the seventy-year-old Holley Hotel. (Owen Stayner)

Highland Park, Michigan. At a senior citizens community meeting during a re-call election campaign, Mayor Robert B. Blackwell discusses his record during twelve years as mayor. He survived his third re-call election to remain mayor of Highland Park. (Fred C. Ferris)

Parma, Ohio. Gymnasium, Saint Charles Catholic School, Ridge Road (Charles P. Cervenak)

Burlington, Vermont. Henry's Diner (Arnold Carbone)

ABOVE
Burlington, Vermont. Patrons attend the Johnny Cash Show at the Flynn Theater, an art deco landmark currently undergoing restoration. (Gary Clayton-Hall)

BELOW
Schenectady, New York. State Street (Spencer W. Birt)

RIGHT
Pittsburgh, Pennsylvania. More than 300 events are held each year in Pittsburgh's Heinz Hall. (R. Keller)

ABOVE
Tempe, Arizona. The Gold Rush, Apache Boulevard (Brian O. Mahoney)

BELOW
Natchez, Mississippi. Under The Hill Saloon, Silver Street (Charles E. Thomas)

PRECEDING PAGES
Buffalo, New York. City Hall (Eugene Charles Stemp)

ABOVE
Bloomington, Indiana. Scene at Jakes, a college bar in Bloomington (Jay Crawford)

BELOW
Augusta, Georgia. Discotheque Lounge, Broad Street (Michael E. Johnson)

CLOCKWISE FROM TOP LEFT

Flint, Michigan. Fisher Body Plant, South Saginaw Street (Philip Henderson)

Carbondale, Illinois. Dairy Queen, South Illinois Street, downtown Carbondale (Mary Beth Nolan)

Tulsa, Oklahoma. The Mid-Continent Tower, South Boston Avenue, downtown Tulsa. (Terence Klein)

Monroe, Louisiana. Olin Hall Dormitory, on the campus of Northeast Louisiana University, is reflected in the Bayou DeSiard (Robert Ragland)

FROM TOP TO BOTTOM

Lakewood, California. This arrest on Palo Verde was staged for a video documentary on the Sky Knight Helicopter Patrol Program. (Bradley Johnson)

Tulsa, Oklahoma. Englin Neou prepares to clean the interior of a Metro Tulsa Transit Authority bus. Neou is a Cambodian who came to the United States in 1976 as a political refugee. Tonight he will service ninety buses. (Steven Barrett)

Cheyenne, Wyoming. The Union Pacific Depot, Capitol Avenue (Cindy Urbigkit)

Taunton, Massachusetts. The Crocker Building (Cathy Faria)

Wauwatosa, Wisconsin. Little Red Store, West Harwood Avenue (James R. Peterson)

ABOVE
Sarasota, Florida. The 888 Harbor, Sarasota City Marina (John Solum)

BELOW
Portland, Maine. Old Port seen from Portland Harbor (Steven C. Davis)

*Macon, Georgia. This revitalized fountain is part of a restoration
project on Cherry Street. (Rita A. Keller)*

ABOVE
Appleton, Wisconsin. Soldier Square (David T. Kunstman)

OVERLEAF
Saint Paul, Minnesota. Mickey's Diner, West 9th Street (J. W. Stegbauer, J. T. Bougie)

AFTERWORD

Compiling a pictorial album of the entire American urban scene, with its vast geographical and cultural differences, initially seemed to me to be an incredibly ambitious and possibly unrealistic undertaking. My husband, however—the eternal optimist—felt certain that the sheer excitement of participating in such a unique and special project would be enough to carry us through.

It seemed apparent that accurately depicting every facet of our great country had to involve a wide range of cities, large and small, rich and poor, industrial and agricultural. By working through the United States Conference of Mayors, we were able to excite and inspire over two hundred cities to get in on the action. It took a lot of doing, but hundreds of letters, phone calls, and questions later, we had all learned a lot about organizing and coordinating such a national effort. I was more than once pleasantly surprised to discover that the first question I was asked by a city was "How do we enter?"

As the project progressed, many cities proved very good at planning for the big day. Out of each mayor's office, coordinating committees were formed and organizations as diverse as arts councils, senior citizens associations, commerce clubs, library councils, and tourism bureaus were put into use for the effort. Many cities took the initiative to produce posters, press releases, talk shows, and public service announcements to build enthusiasm. Local newspapers helped enormously. Consequently, by the time March 20 rolled around and everything had been planned—except for the weather—thousands of citizens seemed eager to "get into the picture."

Getting into the picture meant many different things to different people, but each had the same goal—catching a unique part of life on film. For example, I received a telephone call from a man in California who had spent weeks coordinating the photographing of a birth. He later reported that Mother Nature had cooperated and the birth took place early in the morning of the 20th.

On another occasion, I discovered that a woman in Florida actually bought her very first camera and took classes in photography in order to be ready. Can you imagine her excitement when she learned that her city ranked her photographs first and second in their submission for the book? Stories

Fitchburg to Be a Snap In National Contest

Photo contest seeks slices of Americana

Three judges chosen for photo contest

Photos To Be Taken Today For U.S. Mayors' Project

Today is the day to take that picture of Daly City

Day in life of Key West to be chronicled

National Contest Sponsored By The United States Conference Of Mayors

like these occurred in so many cities that the making of the book became an exciting story in itself.

As it happened, two cities, Hartford, Connecticut, and Wauwatosa, Wisconsin, used the photographs as a part of their 350- and 150-year celebrations, respectively, while many others created their own "book within a book" by printing a twenty-four-hour pictorial history themselves.

Not surprisingly, because the theme of the project was so broad, the responses of the photographers varied enormously. Certain predictable subjects appeared often: early morning and evening, commuter traffic, schoolchildren at street crossings, city hall architecture. A goodly number of coffee shop interiors, barber shops, flag raisings and lowerings, and main street shoppers, testify to the fact that Americans basically eat well, keep themselves groomed, are patriotic, and maintain a consumer society. Happily for the diversity of the images in the book, people brought out their cameras even when the weather was bad. Thus, we learn that on March 20, 1985 it was raining in New Orleans and there was plenty of snow on the ground in Idaho Falls. On the other hand, places blessed with sunshine celebrated that fact, and Maui, Key West, and Santa Barbara unabashedly showed off

their natural good luck. Several photographers paid special attention to the fact that the selected date was the first offical day of spring; several chose to record brand-new or very recent births (and one pictured a funeral); two, at least, recorded the date itself in their pictures—one written in wet cement and another on a school blackboard—and several had the inspiration and foresight to station themselves near clocks to document the first minute of the new day.

In other respects, the photographers did just what we had, I think, hoped they might do, that is, to record the wonderfully varied and average happenings of life in these United States much as it might be lived on any day in the year. Without looking either on a falsely bright side or a gloomily negative one, they saw America plainly. Only one photographer felt it necessary to portray the mayor of his town; only one pictured a political rally; no one shot a city council meeting. While there are several pictures of doctors and nurses, and one judge, most photographs of people at work are of nonprofessionals doing the things that make the country tick.

Photographers and others might like to know how the pictures were selected for the book. First, and appropriately, it was a democratic process—participation meant representation. That is, every city that conducted a competition and submitted its selections was guaranteed to be represented in the book by at least one photograph. We were gratified by the many multiple submissions, which meant that the best could be chosen, though of course one city's pictures might not be nearly so good as another's. Nevertheless, they are each featured here.

An anonymous jury of photographic and design professionals volunteered to judge all the entries—with the proviso that they choose at least one from each entered city. Beyond that, their first choice was for the best photograph in each city's submission, the best being determined by the quality of the photographic image—its composition, lighting, angle of view, subject matter, and conception. Very few technically poor photographs were submitted by the cities, but good exposure and sharp focus (unless the intention was otherwise) were considered basic to all choices.

When the final city-by-city selections were made, a further judging took place that, sadly, eliminated some very good pictures. This was because an ensemble had to be created: pictures from the whole twenty-four-hour span that cumulatively added up to a varied life study of the nation. Thus, for instance, if two very good dawn photographs of commuter traffic were in hand, one might have been eliminated for another picture from the same city at a different time of day and of a different subject. If a photographer from one city submitted an unusually good group of pictures, all may have been chosen, though this meant choosing one less from another city. Considerations of the size or importance of cities figured not at all in the selections; Farmers Branch, Texas, might have ended up with more selections than Philadelphia. Finally, within the constraints of the publisher's limits to the number of pictures that could be contained within the book, the last selections were made.

We've tried to show you on these pages just a glimpse of what happened leading up to March 20th, and I hope you sense, as I have, the electricity that was generated on this day for thousands of photographers across America.

Judith Carver

ACKNOWLEDGMENTS

We would like to thank our publisher, and particularly Bob Morton, who allowed two beginners to complete a project by virtue of his understanding and support; Mr. John Gunther and the staff of the United States Conference of Mayors; and the mayors, coordinators, and the various groups within each city who sponsored and organized the events that caused these photographs to become available.

INDEX OF CITIES

INDEX OF PHOTOGRAPHERS